T0362882

DOROTHY PORTER

OTHER WORLDS

*un*tapped

ABOUT *UNTAPPED*

Most Australian books ever written have fallen out of print and become unavailable for purchase or loan from libraries. This includes important local and national histories, biographies and memoirs, beloved children's titles, and even winners of glittering literary prizes such as the Miles Franklin Literary Award.

Supported by funding from state and territory libraries, philanthropists and the Australian Research Council, *Untapped* is identifying Australia's culturally important lost books, digitising them, and promoting them to new generations of readers. As well as providing access to lost books and a new source of revenue for their writers, the *Untapped* collaboration is supporting new research into the economic value of authors' reversion rights and book promotion by libraries, and the relationship between library lending and digital book sales. The results will feed into public policy discussions about how we can better support Australian authors, readers and culture.

See untapped.org.au for more information, including a full list of project partners and rediscovered books.

Readers are reminded that these books are products of their time. Some may contain language or reflect views that might now be found offensive or inappropriate.

for my sisters, Mary and Josie

CONTENTS

Other Worlds

Comets 8

UFO. 14

Black smoker 15

Disaster 17

Europa 19

My own private prison 20

Snakes and ladders 21

Death 22

Aztecs. 27

Colosseum. 29

Magpie 30

The famous writer. 31

Faith. 32

The pool 34

everything becomes mysterious 35

Kaua'i. 37

Poet in Medellin 38

The Northern Territory

Deadly sea. 47

The inland sea 48

Snake story 50

The stars. 51

Black & white. 52

On request

Torch song for Sydney 54

It's raining diamonds on Neptune 56

Look no hands/one night stand. 57

Calling a spade. 59

Volcano Vertigo. 61

Acknowledgements 65

Copyright 66

OTHER WORLDS

COMETS

I

There's a white—blue nerve burning
across my night sky

I wish it hurt to watch

because then
    I might stop.

II

In my brain scan
is a white bullet

what will it plug
for my birthday?

Every year I ask for
less of the same

every year I ask for
a fiery surprise.

III

What voice of dirty ice
is talking in my head?

I can't watch the sky
without ringing Heaven.

My heart ticking as slowly
as poison
over its hissing dial tone.

Pick up, Heaven.
Please pick up.

It's me.

IV

I pray for
a virulent visitor

my body fluids rushing
        to meet it

I'll replicate
        replicate

my celestial virus.

V

When the Earth passed through
the vaporous tail of the comet

you were there

it rained forty days
and forty nights
on your uplifted face.

Someone was there
enjoying you

they passionately
took your photo

I'm looking at it now.

Thank God
for rain.

Thank God
for comets.

VI

A comet processed
as a negative
is black.

Space is white
with melanoma spots
for stars.

Let me end in fire
on a night of low smog
bright on the horizon.

Will my lips stream
a black tail?

VII

Cats and comets
are cousins.

With arching tails
and bright orbiting
mating swoops.

I used to sleep
hugging my cat.

I used to sleep
my nose buried
in her fur.

Now I wake up
seared happy
a bull's-eye scorched
right through my chest.

VIII

I'm finished
with generously swerving
into barren arms

and fostering out
my bacteria babies.

I don't trust you
anymore
childless planets.

There's no milk
in your irradiated
old tits.

There's celibate cruelty
in your trap
of dusty craters
and thin gas gruel.

You only grow to hate
and abuse
my cheeky scum.

IX

After sunset
above the horizon
near the hunched bright arch
of the Westgate Bridge

through binoculars
shivering

you looked looked looked.

But what difference
does the looking
of a finite terrestrial
neurally-aglow mammal
really make?

Let your own watery
chemistry's delusions

boil
for a pulsing moment.

And believe
your squinting eyes
your warm breath
keep this fuzzy speck
    blazing in and out
    of the night clouds
going.

X

Stop trying to remember
the swarming pong
off extinct broth.

Stop scuttling obsessively
through antique shellgrit.

Stand
in the comet's
blue tickling tail.

Snag its fever.

UFO

Let
words fail you
when they arrive
exhausted
blinded by the alien
shine of water and sky

for all their unimaginable
superiority
you will terrify them

the shine of your eyes
the blinding gabble
of your curiosity.

BLACK SMOKER

trench
it's your grandfather's word
not yours

it means the smell
of entrails in mud

it means war.

trench
you want to tell his ghost
the news

trench
means life,
life wriggling
like a grilled maggot
from a scorching nowhere.

You try and describe
a friendly hell
in an ocean trench
in loving reach
of an oozing vent
where hot water shocks
into cold

and black smokers
streaming locks of tube worms
grow.

It makes you wonder,
you ask your grandfather,
about the fertility
of other hells—

the chattering pregnancy
in every misery.

DISASTER

for Diane Lightfoot

Why is it so fascinating
watching disaster's colonies
grow?

Some hang before the mouth
like clusters of grapes,
others wriggle
like the tempting blips
of distant constellations.

Is the microscope honest?
Is the Petri dish safe?

Disaster can be
so gentle on the eye,
wondrously translucent
a swimming mystery
with delicate working
parts.

It's not so easy
calling you names,
disaster.

Even when the lid
is lifted
on your putrid stink

you are generously
enlightening us
to the real world

its luridly lovely movie,
Divide and Rule.

EUROPA

No wonder you love
Europa.

You will never crack
the crust
of this blinding ice moon
and dredge its slush.

If its thin cold air
could ever fizz
in brave human lungs
you would still be the last
to breathe it.

You're happy
for Europa
to stay in its remote orbit
showering down
the odd twinkling tick
to squat in your skin.

So much easier
to scratch its itch
and laze
   in enigma

than love
   and render to
the drunk woman
   in blinding distress
dirtying your street.

MY OWN PRIVATE PRISON

I thought I could own everything
until I knew I'd never own that strange emerald thing—
another's suffering.

I thought I'd never see my treasure chest
grinning with green growing pain.

I hankered for the dank touch, the fungus smell,
top of the range suffering.

Where but behind the night soil smell of locks
and loss
can the profit plant grow truly lush?

Who will let me buy
a yard of suffering?

Who will let me buy
my own private prison?

SNAKES AND LADDERS

There's a mind-bite to be
scratched.
My fingernails are useless.

I have to live with it
this red spot, like Jupiter's,
full of stupendous lightning
whirling itch.

My snake can charm
rivers of thought
uphill.

In trance you drink
miracles.

I climb the ladder
and scratch the snake
    swallowing my head.

DEATH

I

Cure death's skin
till it smells like leather
and feels like chamois.

Wear it this winter.

Just
    don't let the corpse
        get up
            and wear you.

II

You're forty-five
When are you going to learn
    discretion?

For once
hold your tongue.

Don't rush
to tell death
    everything.

III

The skulls of your comrades
glow in the candlelight

glow pinkly
as they carouse

it's been a good night

lots of drink
lots of drugs
lots of sex
    (or talk of it)

but it's too late
  for you

way past your blurring
  bedtime.

IV

Stepping over the threshold
of an old photograph

you're sneezing
dead faces

you want to scratch
the paper

until something
squeaks.

V

Does envy die
too?

Does *post mortem* envy
balloon with its own gas
and rot?

Or does envy survive
everything

and glow
like a post-holocaust
cockroach
with horrifying health?

VI

Every moment
is death's waiting room

you can bob
on the diamond-chip river
one moment
like a pelican

but the moment may move

inexorably
to the next
where you're waiting,
like Lorca
flayed of poetry

in a silent room,
with rust in your gut
waiting
for a man
all beak and claw
to call you in.

VII

for Jennifer Harrison

You can't sleep off
this last pea on your plate
that might dart to your breast
and grow

you lie stiff
and your breath chokes
as you approach
the tangling kingdom
of empty palaces
where everything tastes
of autumn.

Sleep sweet.

Listen to your own blood
        like the sea.
And eat that pea.

VIII

for Emma

And at the end
perhaps
there'll be a straggling
smell

a smell
of eye-watering
summer

a smell
purring
along the bluestone lane

one last trick
one last leap
   of roses.

AZTECS

Show him the marvel.
May he desire, may he long for
the flowery death
by the obsidian knife.

Aztec hymn

If you're longing to know
 the Feathered Snake,
if you long to live
 by its rules,
remember this:

Learn to love cruelty.

You can't shy
 from the splash of blood,
or its terrible smell oozing
 under the screaming of children.

You're nobly nourished
 inside this sacred moment,
like a young wasp
 eating through the guts
of its inferior paralysed host.

But when the priests
 of your own true faith
light a fire
 on the living skin

of your palpitating heart
    don't cry out.

Honour is cruelty's
    most insatiable bedmate,
your pride must always
    keep its own fires burning
even if, note this,
    your own heart must die.

COLOSSEUM

What am I trying to feed
over and beyond
the urgent callousness
of sore feet, parched throat?

What fagged-out fake
actress in me
is posing spooked
before these tourist-smooth
ruins
as benign as a crumbling
wasp's nest?

I can smell—
thick air, urine—
        lion?

Present tense.
Stifling crowd. Pregnant cat.

Eventually the past gives
us up.

Even that fixed immortal moment
on all fours. howl. spout of bright red blood.
will, in the froth of time,
tip us out.

MAGPIE

Memory is a nesting magpie
it dives for my eyes
when the red gums
are blossoming
when memory's eggs
are hatching

my heart hammers
under a tree
roosting shadows

I want eyes in the back of my head
because memory is remembering
because memory wants me dead.

THE FAMOUS WRITER

His thoughts are banal
time flies   so much water under the bridge
as he talks in an elegant monologue
to the women at his table

his thoughts are banal
as he watches his old lover
across the room clutching
a slopping glass of red
his old lover's face flushed clownish
as he corners a much younger man
with inarticulate passion and
another round of drinks

the famous writer tries to remember
his old lover's last book
he tries to remember
other older more intimate things
it's like trying to remember
a bog as a bower

the famous writer is sober
he has to be these days
his hands are elegantly talking
his thoughts are banal
so much so much   time   under the bridge
watching his old lover

FAITH

I've lived a life
illuminated and
choked
by dreaming

sometimes everything
threads together
in a lightning-charred
tapestry
almost too exciting
to contemplate
let alone live with

other times
have left me
stranded and sobbing
in a muggy black night
of longing
and plain bloody nonsense

but best of all
dreaming
has left a dusting
of memory-mushed images

doesn't matter
if they can rear at me
like the legs of the frozen
dead donkey
I saw sticking out
stiff

in an otherwise
serenely barren desert

they burn and smelt
this world, this life
into great messy
plundering sense.

THE POOL

'Am I really a note or a flower?'

Anna Akhmatova

There's nothing throw-away
    about an iguana
        or this enchantment

I slip,
    with an iguana's cold-blooded
        hungry nerve,
into a pool
    struck hot and dumb
        by lightning.

And lose.
    Lose thermostat.
        Lose skin.
            And then, only then,
                I can sing.

EVERYTHING BECOMES MYSTERIOUS

(Rilke)

is mystery as hard won
as self knowledge?

those eerily lovely
ethane moments
when you're utterly comfortable
with not knowing
the hour, the night, the lesson
or (wonderful ignorance),
the intoxicating face

how did you earn them?

but confess it's the dark matter
of your own soul
its dense invisible gravitational
pull
that really takes your breath
away

one night
you dream of extinct animals
mega-fauna menacing
and fascinating
rising like a flood
from the torrent
of your own furious
thoughts

the animals multiply
and swarm
in a squall of amphibious jaws,
bright green skins
and thylacine stripes

and you flow welcome
and unwelcome
into the awesome glitter
of their galaxy, their terrifying
arrival.

KAUA'I

for Andy

We're drinking tropical cocktails
in the rain

but not getting wet

the rain falls heavily
around us
like a tent of humid hair

we're sitting dry
inside its noisy cool
benevolence

this is paradise.
slightly pissed.
watching the sea and the mountain
moving in and out
through the mist
like our own strange souls.

POET IN MEDELLIN

for Judy

1

Gran Hotel

Poverty looks beautiful,
like a galaxy of hot young stars,
at night
when the barrio clinging to the mountain
twinkles.

2

There was no thief
    in my room.
My things are safe.
What did I need
    to get stolen?

3

My fear is a landslide.

Why did I take its road
    so recklessly
and bump bump
    over its rocks?

4

At night
I close the slats
and listen to the fan
moving the moist equatorial air

by morning
I'm twitching
to walk through
that low grey dangerous sky
again.

5

Inaugural Night Poetry Reading Teatro Carlos Vieco

Their skins glisten
under the smoking moon
as if listening to poetry
was polishing them
into emeralds—

    these uncut students
    this hot diesel-scented night
    clouding in my head
    like a shaman's narcotic.

6

The boy's eyes flutter
    narcotically
as he sways on his feet.
I cannot flow
into his trance
        his salvation *amiga*.
I'm scared stiff.

7

Jardin Botanico Joaquin Antonio Uribe

Vultures circling
    the Botanical Gardens
are waiting for
    that most exquisite of azaleas
(no, not the red one)
    the subtle lead one
    to open its petals
        and release its scent of carrion.

Even on a Sunday
    it may open,
a Sunday
    of children, a sweet breeze
    and church bells,
        especially church bells.

8

Every reading is a ceremony
for the Korean poet
decked out in a red and white
traditional dress
of gruesomely stiff cotton—

before commanding the stage
she walks
equally ceremoniously
five or six steps
behind her husband.

9

The red
The red bird
The cardinal!

Each new name
is a spurt on
like a tadpole's gills
shrivelling
into leaping lungs.

10

Barrio Santa Cruz

What is smoking
  so languidly
on the mountain's eerie side?

Does real danger
  begin like this—
with a picturesque distraction?

11

Cultural Centre Barrio Santa Cruz

A girl's ghost dreamily
whirls on the old brothel's
dancing floor.

What music
can still enslave the dead
to the monotony
  of an old joy?

12

Calle 54

A street vendor
waves her grubby wand
over a basket
of freshly sliced avocados

and their lusciously hollowed flesh
   is a bur in our eyes
    too much delicious green

we rub our eyes
like Verlaine trying to make
his glass of demon-green absinthe
appear bottomless.

13

On the leper's waving stump
is a dab of white ointment.

Is it a potion from a lizard
to make his limb grow back?

14

Hospital Mental. Municipio De Bello

The bust of Sigmund Freud
glows with a greenish metallic
kindliness
outside the white-washed walls
of the mental hospital

while the patients mill,
some with faces like crushed walnuts
others with *otro mundo* stares
waiting for the poets
to read with real matches.

Afterwards a manic reporter
pesters the poets
to define poetry as madness

the interview dissolves
in a shouting discord
of patients defining themselves
over the muted poets.

15

Parque De San Antonio

In Parque de San Antonio
they planted a bomb
in a giant metal bird

and when the bird exploded
that stopped the party
that finished the dancing

the sky rained one vendor's
peanuts and lottery tickets
for a week.

But two nights ago
in Parque de San Antonio
Poetry planted a bomb
in a word.

What will blast to bits
this time?
And who will kick-start
the dancing?

16

Is there a nightingale
under my tenth-floor window
on my last morning in Medellin?

I only know nightingales
from Keats.

But if it is just a humble
Colombian urban dove
bless me with Keatsian soul
enough to listen.

I too have been standing
in the alien corn
waiting in this hallucination city
for the magic casements
to open.

Did I wake or sleep?

THE NORTHERN TERRITORY

DEADLY SEA

What is the brain coral
dreaming
in the warm deep
of this deadly sea?

I creep its soft white sand
my left knee
catching the edge
of every dozing rock.

The water is a gorgeous
lulling aqua
tugging like the taboo mouth
of the woman
you can't swim in.

This sea has been so patient.

It has serenely
filed its nails
it has resisted looking
at its watch
or sighing.

It has always known
I was on my way.

THE INLAND SEA

The new shopping mall
glitters wretchedly
in the desert town

dry river beds
lead crookedly
to dry gorges

we're learning
you can't drink air conditioning.

In every pale plump face
is the gaunt map
of red thirsty bone

but we're rich
and we're fairly
comfortable

don't rescue us
yet.

There are ghosts here
who stink of water

we'll interrogate them
shortly.

Don't worry
we'll make them
tell us

we'll make them
show us
that infuriatingly close

smell-over-the-hill
inland sea.

SNAKE STORY

Death adder,
will I ever learn
when to step on you?

In the dark
I can smell your rustling
dry mulch home

but I can't smell you.

Are you waiting?

How do I shed
this fusty skin of fear
and walk
with artfully reckless
bared ankles?

There's so much honour
in the benediction
of your dream-deep venom.

THE STARS

The oldest dream
is the black tar dream

your throat fills with it
while you sleep

your bones dream
of a mired eternity

your bones dream
of thick, steady sinking.

The stars are old
emetics

they'll speed
down your gullet
like a bright needle
punch.

Take
the terrifying medicine
and vomit yourself
free.

BLACK & WHITE

There's red dirt on my worn boots
where I paced the floor
of an inland sea.

I smelt the red breath
of extinct sharks.

Where have I been?

Was it a riled living snake
knew me
knew my number
and bit?

There's a friendless place
of distinctly rational
distinctly historical
black & white
where no living colour
will ever stray.

Is that my Melbourne
on this cloudy day?

I'm still treading
dust water.

What warm emerald acid
has fanged out
my heart's eye?

ON REQUEST

TORCH SONG FOR SYDNEY

Commissioned by the City of Sydney for the arrival of the
Olympic Torch 14 September 2000

Sharks and yachts.

Sydney's hungriest, most dazzling
flowers
grow on water

but tonight Sydney
will flower on fire.

Tonight a flame will flare
like a swimmer
off the blocks,
burn
like the lungs
of a marathon runner,
at the hearth
of our glittering city.

For once
we welcome fire—

not the stink black fire
that rears like a snake
in summer
and goes for our throats—

we welcome bright fire
that has run like a song-line

through this fierce
and sacred land

passed as a spirit-torch,
glittering
from hand to hand.

IT'S RAINING DIAMONDS ON NEPTUNE

for my cousin Samuel Lawrence on the occasion of his
Naming Day

It's raining diamonds on Neptune
red ice is burning hot and cold
on the Martian poles

there are sulphur spouting volcanoes
bursting like balloons
on Io, Jupiter's fiery
juvenile delinquent moon

while life as we don't know it
swims and draws slow water-rich
breath
in the submarine sea
under the ice of Europa.

But this afternoon
amongst partying blood
we celebrate an earthly
more intimate marvel

we hand over to Samuel,
our new kinsman,
the reins of his name.

LOOK NO HANDS/ONE NIGHT STAND

Commissioned for the anthology Dick For a Day

Just for tonight
  my hands don't matter
just for tonight
  I'm no lesbian
just for tonight
  my hands work for me

no longer
  a nourishing girl
    all wholemeal fingers

no longer
  playing ache to get

tonight
  I'm a hot man
    not scared of the dark

tonight
  I'm a reef shark
    cruising the coral park

I won't touch
    won't touch

I'll watch
  my own moving
    piston self

my hands
　　still
my hands
　　miraculously relaxed

or just flickering
　　on the bones
　　　　of my hips

one hand may stray
　　across the back
　　　　of the strange neck
　　　　　　bent over my axe

or maybe not

because tonight
　　my hands don't matter

because tonight
　　my hands work for me.

CALLING A SPADE

for Barbara Baynton

Commissioned for the anthology Storykeepers

There are no ghouls
just gutless human fools.

And too many, depressing thousands
of female mugs
hanging unlovely
from male hooks.

Barbara, thank you,
you took the 'ess'
out of this romantic poetess.

I will never believe again
in the pioneering spirit,
the magnetic ambiguity
of strangers
or the yearning mischief
of a tender blow.

Now if I must portray the bush
he's just a creeping vagrant
who turns snake-nasty at night
with a nose
for a bullied woman.

Only ask mongrel dogs
for love and loyalty.

But no dog's warm muzzle
can nuzzle you to your feet
from the wreck of dumped
and the lying-in-muck
of a broken back.

Forget the solace of nature.
It's a rustling void
that spills into your heart
the drink you will never forget.
Loneliness.
Best drunk chilled.
With a sprig of grime.

VOLCANO VERTIGO

Commissioned by the Sydney Morning Herald *for*
Summer Fiction *1998*

Hanging By A Thread

'We still have our moments,' he says
pushing off his gas mask,
as he stands cocked at the crater's lip
in the sulphurous breath of the volcano.

She's happy behind her mask
breathing evenly,
shut up shut up shut up shut up
her heart a spitting mud.

There's no poison as paralysing as a holiday
gone wrong.
She almost wishes she was scared
of heights.

A thermal vent wheezes foully behind them,
she thinks of the Earth in its chundering infancy,
she smells the blisters of her marriage's raw heel
bursting.

He talks and talks shaping his hands
into cones and craters,
his fingers she once unimaginably craved for
play the eruptions.

The steam and stink frame his face

in a hellish acrid glamour,
she can almost remember
what she once saw in him.

And what does he really see of her
as he bores on about sulphur-gorging germs
thriving in temperatures
that would fry any other mug living thing?

What would kill her?
Or is she slowly dying anyway
in cooling bits and pieces?
What would kill him?

He's parroting for the third time
the suicide tale the goggle-eyed guide told.
The miner gone missing. His mates' sus story.
The boots left goodbyed on the crater's edge.

She looks with fresh interest
at her husband's cherished runners.
Watches his restless toes
rippling their grubby leather.

And sees them still and empty.
Sooty, wreathed in steam.
Happily coupled
as only inanimate objects can be.

She has a flash clear memory
of a tiny empty flat,
and her own things happily strewn
in their own solitary clutter.

Oh, Christ, she was learning

there were worse horrors than loneliness,
as he jumps about like a cricket
his camera clicking her masked averted face.

Would she catch the volcano fever
if it were Stephen's finger on the trigger,
if it were Stephen's toes rippling the runners?
Would her heart's magma rush to his whistle?

Stephen. She barely knows him.
Stephen. An ageing woman's sticky fantasy.
Stephen. Should she send him a postcard?
Of a volcano. Spewing up its sad old guts.

Stephen's long-distance enticements evaporate
as her husband grabs her arm,
she's dreamily moved too close to the edge
'I don't want to lose you ... yet!'

Extinct. Extinct. Extinct.
A volcano's death knell sounds her own.
Or is she just itchy dormant
awaiting her big eruptive moment?

Watch Stephen charring
in her own last fling Ring of Fire.
Let them lie down and die together
in her deepest hissing fumarole.

Her husband wipes his excited hands
on his silly white shorts,
and she prays for a lava bomb
to gouge him away.

'Are you a praying mantis
about to munch on her mate?'
he jokes, and yanks
at the ridiculous nose of her mask.

don't touch don't touch me
the volcano was bringing out
the randy pest in him,
he'd be buzzing all night.

'Wouldn't the kids find this place wicked!'
and he starts moronically singing,
as if he can't stand the volcano
getting all the attention.

Caldera Lullaby

She's humming her own tune
as the boat glides away,
an ash plume climbing
into the late afternoon sky.

And blessing her lump
of lucky sulphur,
and blessing the luck
of hazy head counts.

ACKNOWLEDGEMENTS

I would like to thank the following magazines, anthologies and editors, especially Ivor Indyk, for their support: *Heat; Meanjin; Southerly; Cordite; My One True Love* (edited by Caro Llewellyn, Random House); the *Age;* the *Atlanta Review* (USA); the *Prague Review;* the *Bulletin; Verandah; Prism International* (Canada); *Dick For a Day* (edited by Fiona Giles, Random House); *Storykeepers* (edited by Marion Halligan, Allen & Unwin); Vagabond Press (with special thanks to Michael Brennan) and the *Sydney Morning Herald.*

I would also like to thank the English Department at Melbourne University for my Honorary Fellowship, which has been of great assistance in the writing and researching of a number of these poems.

And my grateful thanks to two fine writers for their editorial expertise: firstly, my friend, the poet Judith Beveridge, and finally my partner, Andrea Goldsmith, for not only her acute critical eye but also her love and support.

COPYRIGHT

Copyright © Dorothy Porter 2001

First published in 2001 by Picador

This electronic edition published in 2019 by Ligature Pty Limited.
34 Campbell St · Balmain NSW 2041 · Australia
www.ligatu.re · mail@ligatu.re

e-book ISBN: 9781925883145

All rights reserved. Except as provided by fair dealing or any other
exception to copyright, no part of this book may be reproduced or
transmitted in any form or by any means without permission in
writing from the publisher.

The author asserts her moral rights throughout the world without
waiver.

This print edition published in collaboration with Brio Books,
an imprint of Booktopia Group Ltd

Level 6, 1A Homebush Bay Drive · Rhodes NSW 2138 · Australia

Print ISBN: 9781761281020

briobooks.com.au

The paper in this book is FSC® certified.
FSC® promotes environmentally responsible,
socially beneficial and economically viable
management of the world's forests.